✳ Basic Rules ✳

 Fold in the reverse directon of the dotted line. This is known as the 'mountain' fold.

Fold alor in the di arrow. This is called the 'valley' fold.

MW00343004

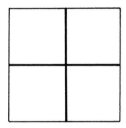

Cut 1 sheet into 4 equal parts.

①

②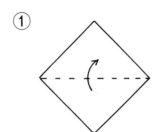

③

④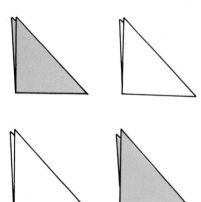

Fold 2 quarter-sheets so that the colored side is on the outside, and 2 sheets with the color on the inside.

⑤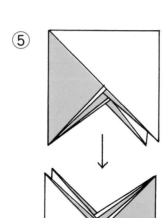

First, make 2 pairs by inserting the colored pieces into the white pieces as shown in the diagram and then put these 2 halves together as shown in 6.

⑥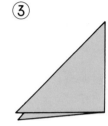

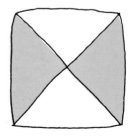

Finished

BIRD (MOBILE)

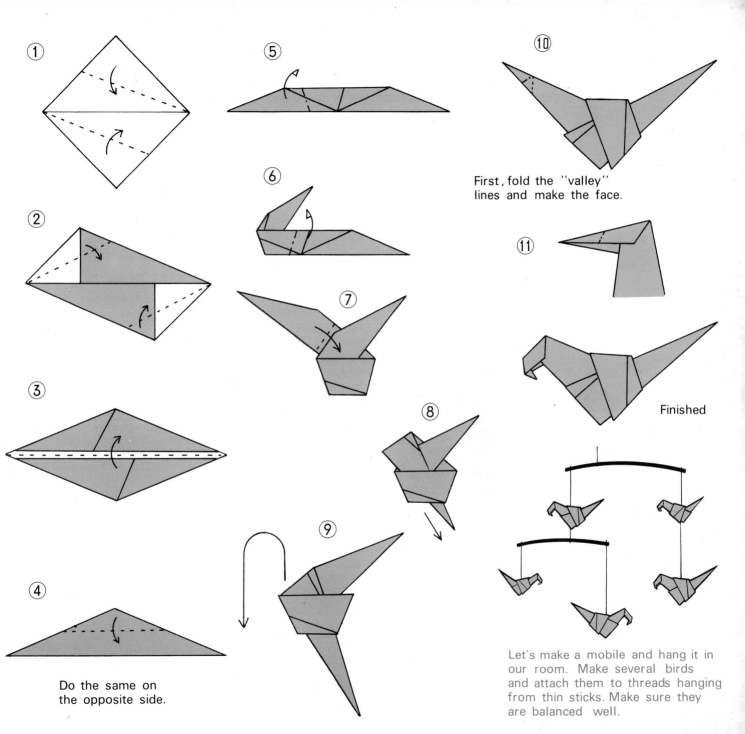

① ⑤ ⑩

First, fold the "valley"
lines and make the face.

② ⑥ ⑪

③ ⑦ Finished

④ ⑧

Do the same on
the opposite side.

⑨

Let's make a mobile and hang it in
our room. Make several birds
and attach them to threads hanging
from thin sticks. Make sure they
are balanced well.

WITCH

WITCH

Make creases following the arrows in steps 1-4 and open the paper.

①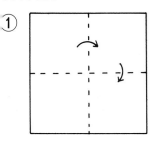

②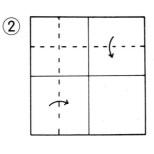

③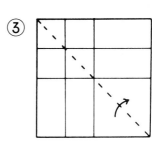

④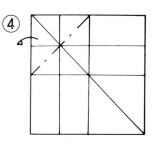

⑤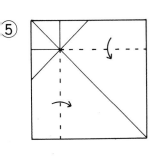

⑥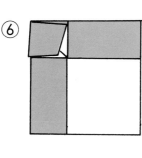

⑦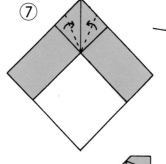

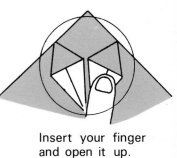

Insert your finger and open it up.

⑧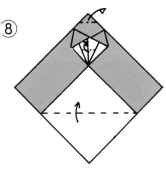

⑨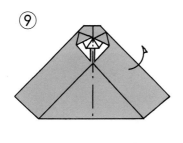

⑩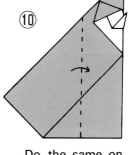

Do the same on the opposite side.

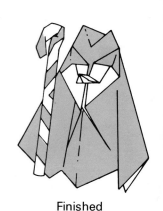

Finished

STAFF

①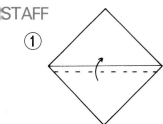

Make a fold a little below the center line.

②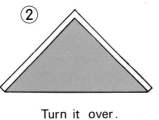

Turn it over.

③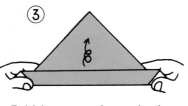

Fold it up as shown in the diagram and paste the end.

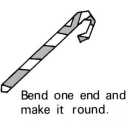

Bend one end and make it round.

SEA GULL

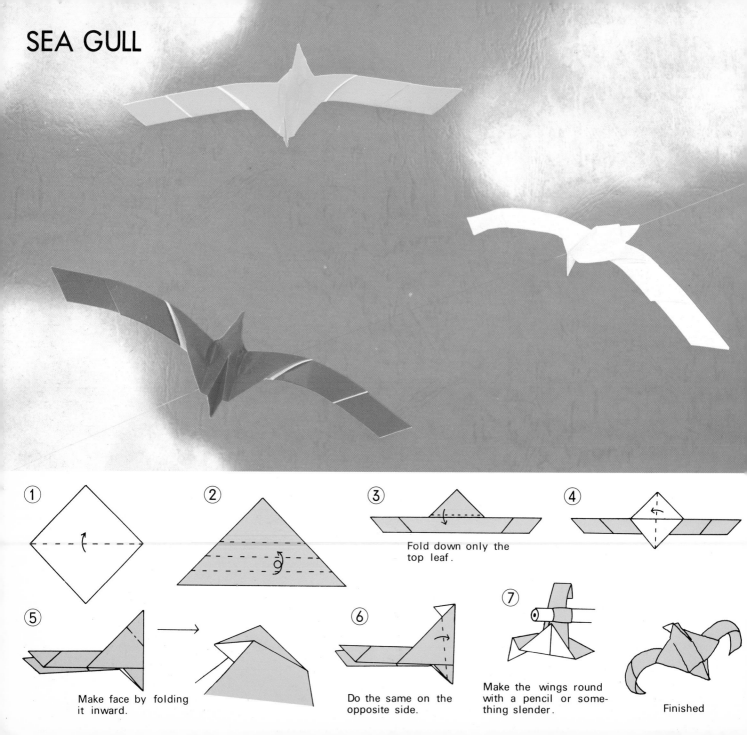

①

②

③ Fold down only the top leaf.

④

⑤ Make face by folding it inward.

⑥ Do the same on the opposite side.

⑦ Make the wings round with a pencil or something slender.

Finished

SWAN

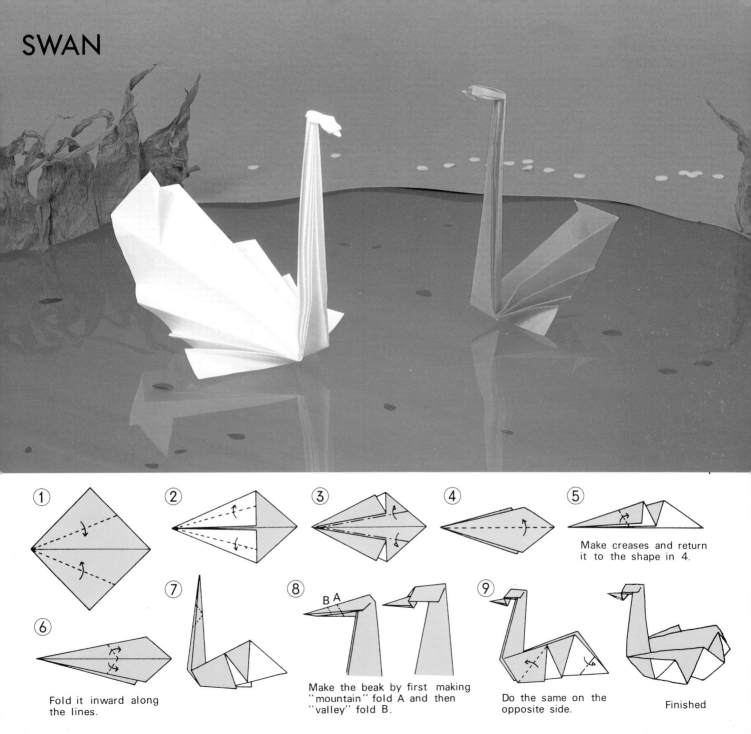

①

②

③

④

⑤ Make creases and return it to the shape in 4.

⑥ Fold it inward along the lines.

⑦

⑧ Make the beak by first making "mountain" fold A and then "valley" fold B.

B A

⑨ Do the same on the opposite side.

Finished

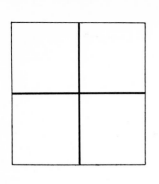

Cut the paper into 4 parts.

③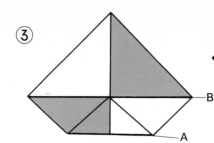

B

A

Fold line A up to
Line B.

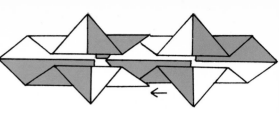

Make many of the same forms
and paste them together as
shown in the diagram.

①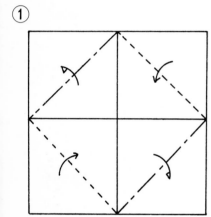

④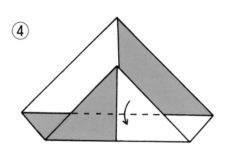

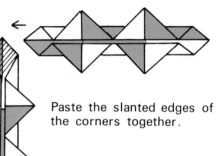

Paste the slanted edges of
the corners together.

⑤

Fold the upper half in the
same way as in steps 2-5.

②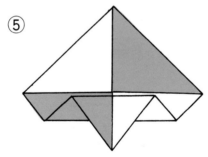

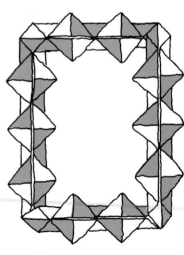

Finished

Paste a thick sheet of paper on
the back-side of the frame and
insert your favorite photographs
or drawings.

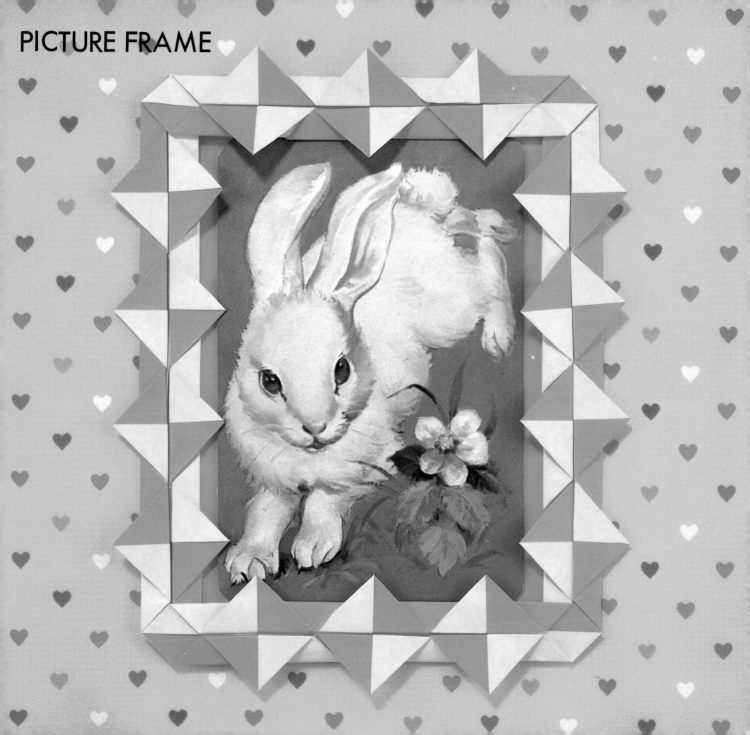

PICTURE FRAME

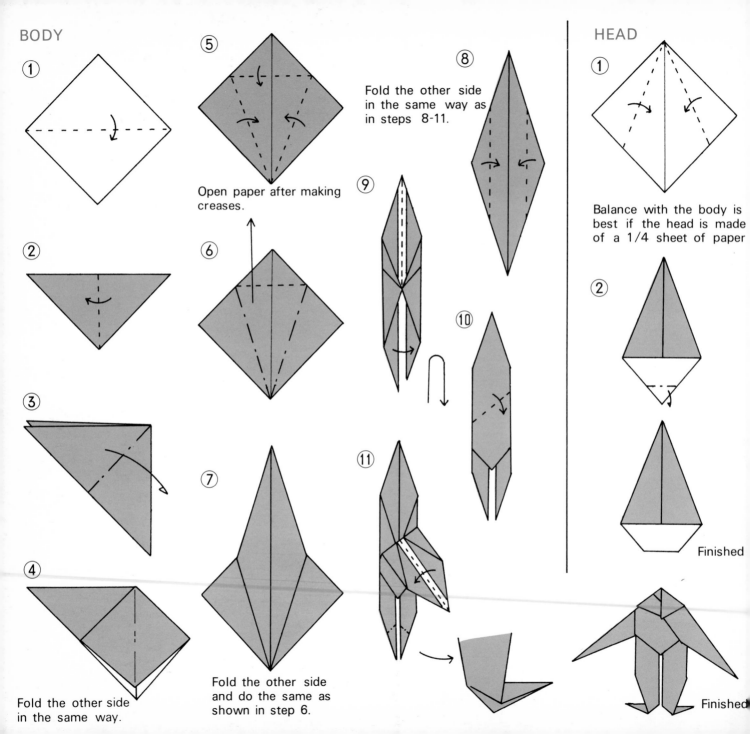

BODY

①

②

③

④

Fold the other side in the same way.

⑤ Open paper after making creases.

⑥

⑦ Fold the other side and do the same as shown in step 6.

⑧ Fold the other side in the same way as in steps 8-11.

⑨

⑩

⑪

HEAD

① Balance with the body is best if the head is made of a 1/4 sheet of paper

②

Finished

Finished

ELF

MONKEY

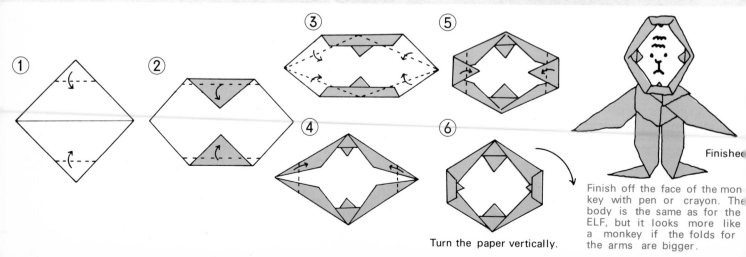

① ② ③ ④ ⑤ ⑥

Turn the paper vertically.

Finished

Finish off the face of the monkey with pen or crayon. The body is the same as for the ELF, but it looks more like a monkey if the folds for the arms are bigger.